ZOOM IN!

Visual Illusions and Guessing games

An Hachette UK Company
www.hachette.co.uk

First published in Great Britain in 2014 by Ticktock,
an imprint of Octopus Publishing Group Ltd
Endeavour House
189 Shaftesbury Avenue
London
WC2H 8JY
www.octopusbooks.co.uk
www.ticktockbooks.co.uk

ISBN 978 1 78325 142 1

A CIP record for this book is available from the British Library.

Printed and bound in China

1 3 5 7 9 10 8 6 4 2

Commissioning Editor: Anna Bowles
Publisher: Samantha Sweeney
Senior Production Manager: Peter Hunt
Production Controller: Sarah-Jayne Johnson

Picture credits:
Every effort has been made to trace the copyright holders, and we apologise in advance for any
unintentional omissions. We would be pleased to insert the appropriate acknowledgement in any
subsequent edition of this publication.
Magnifying glass - Shutterstock.com/musicman, 1, 4br, 15 Shutterstock.com/mycteria, 1b, 41b Shutterstock.com/Eric Isselee, 2-3,
10 Shutterstock.com/argus, 3t, 5bl Shutterstock.com/Marty Pitcairn, endpapers, 3bl, 11 Shutterstock.com/bubu45, 3br, 5br, 13, 47
Shutterstock.com/aquariagirl1970, 4, 8, 18, 32 Shutterstock.com/Apostrophe, 4cl, 29t Shutterstock.com/Marc Parsons, 4cr
Shutterstock.com/Subbotina Anna, 4bl, 39 Shutterstock.com/Venus Angel, 5tc, 45 Shutterstock.com/Gurgen Bakhshetsyan, 5tl, 6b
Shutterstock.com/Tomatito, 5tr, 31 Shutterstock.com/Mazzzur, 5cl, 17tr Shutterstock.com/Borja Andreu, 6t Shutterstock.com/Michal
Ninger, 7 Shutterstock.com/Tumanyan, 7t Shutterstock.com/Kletr, 7b Shutterstock.com/Joao Pedro Silva, 8t Shutterstock.com/
Tatiana Makotra, 8b Shutterstock.com/Rolf E. Staerk, 9 Shutterstock.com/Marc Parsons, 10c Shutterstock.com/
StevenRussellSmithPhotos, 12c Shutterstock.com/Viktar Malyshchyts, 14 Shutterstock.com/apiguide, 16 Shutterstock.com/Norph,
16c Shutterstock.com/Igor Kovalchuk, 17tl Shutterstock.com/Steven M. Ross, 17bl Shutterstock.com/Jim Barber, 17br Shutterstock.
com/mygoodpix, 18tl Shutterstock.com/Dan Thornberg, 18tr Shutterstock.com/Aaron Amat, 18bl Shutterstock.com/DeanHarty, 18br
Shutterstock.com/Robyn Mackenzie, 19 Shutterstock.com/Artography, 20 Shutterstock.com/Brian A Jackson, 21 Shutterstock.com/
ZiZ7StockPhotos, 22c Shutterstock.com/kamnuan, 23 Shutterstock.com/Lizard, 24 Shutterstock.com/tiverylucky, 25 Shutterstock.
com/Jomwaschara Komvorn, 26, 29, 36 Shutterstock.com/argus, 26b Shutterstock.com/PardoY, 27 Shutterstock.com/chaoss, 28
Shutterstock.com/Eric Isselee, 29b Shutterstock.com/Stefanie Mohr Photography, 30 Shutterstock.com/Andreev Alexey, 30t
Shutterstock.com/Dan Kosmayer, 30b Shutterstock.com/vitor costa, 32c Shutterstock.com/Melica, 33 Shutterstock.com/gresei, 34
Shutterstock.com/andreasnikolas, 35 Shutterstock.com/zhuhe2343603, 36 Shutterstock.com/noppharat, 37 Shutterstock.com/
MikeNG, 38 Shutterstock.com/Gordon Bell, 40 Shutterstock.com/Africa Studio, 41tl Shutterstock.com/Andaman, 41tr Shutterstock.
com/optimarc, 42t Shutterstock.com/almondd, 42bl Shutterstock.com/Tom linster, 42br Shutterstock.com/Eric Isselee, 43
Shutterstock.com/Imageman, 44 Shutterstock.com/Maxim Petrichuk, 46 Shutterstock.com/Ian 2010, 48 Shutterstock.com/grafvision

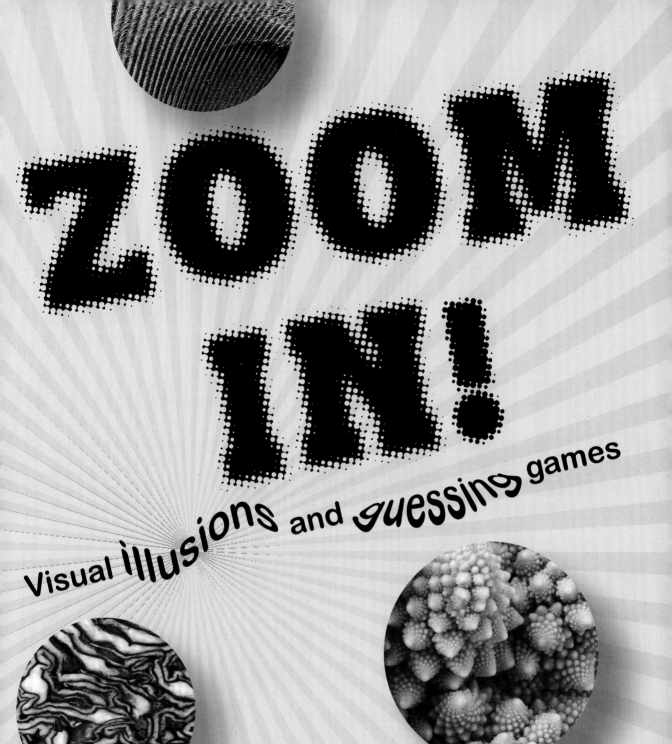

ZOOM IN!

Visual illusions and guessing games

Ticktock

Seeing is... confusing!

Things can look bizarre when you see them very close up. Turn the pages to find out what these odd-looking objects are.

Eyes surprise

What curious creatures have peepers like these?

Answers at the bottom of page 8.

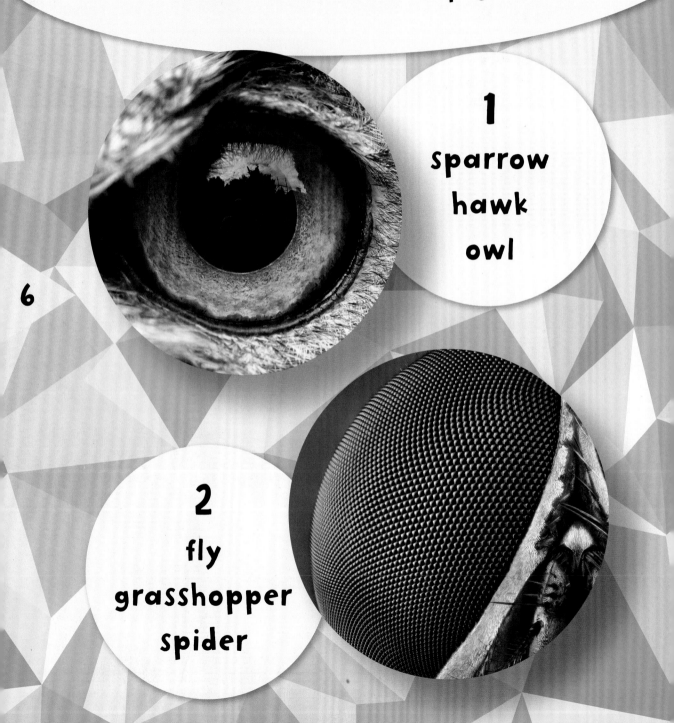

1
sparrow
hawk
owl

6

2
fly
grasshopper
spider

3
alligator
fly
fish

4
sheep
squid
fish

5
chimp
fish
human

8

6
alligator
shark
chameleon

9

Soft and
silky-smooth!
But what is it?
Are those tiny stitches?
How do they glow
so bright?

The biggest butterfly is the Queen Alexandra's Birdwing, which can measure 30 cm across. It's the jumbo jet of the insect world!

It's a butterfly!

The amazing colours are created by tiny scales that scatter light. The effect is pretty to us, pretty to the butterfly's mate, and often scary to predators.

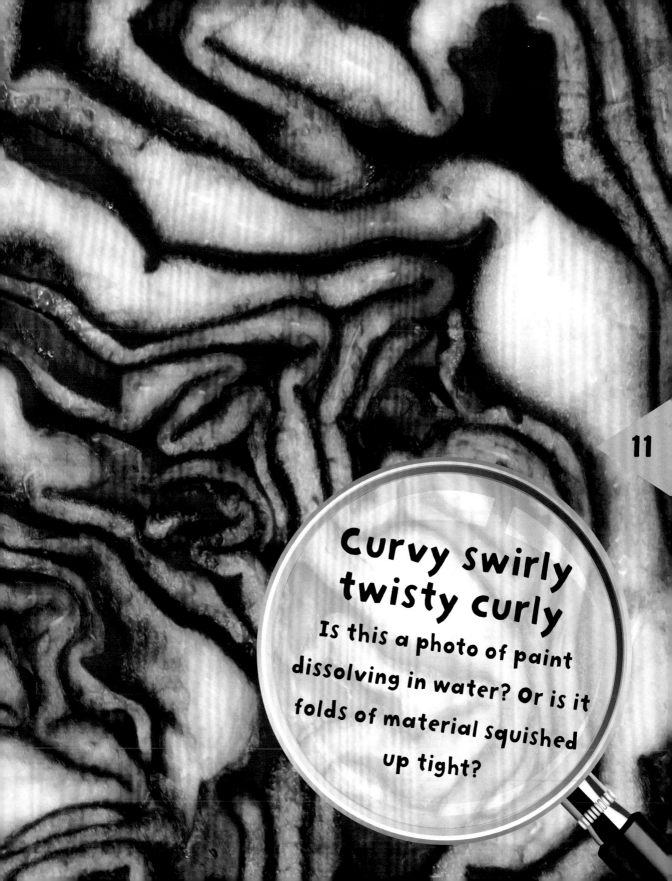

Curvy swirly twisty curly

Is this a photo of paint dissolving in water? Or is it folds of material squished up tight?

The largest cabbage meal ever was made in 2008 in Macedonia and consisted of 80,191 cabbage rolls. Yummy...

It's red cabbage!

The swirling patterns are made by tightly packed leaves. Cabbages grow by adding layer after layer of them until there are dozens all squashed together.

13

It's grass
growing on a
rainbow!
OK, that's not true. But what
is it, then? A tapestry?
A woven basket?

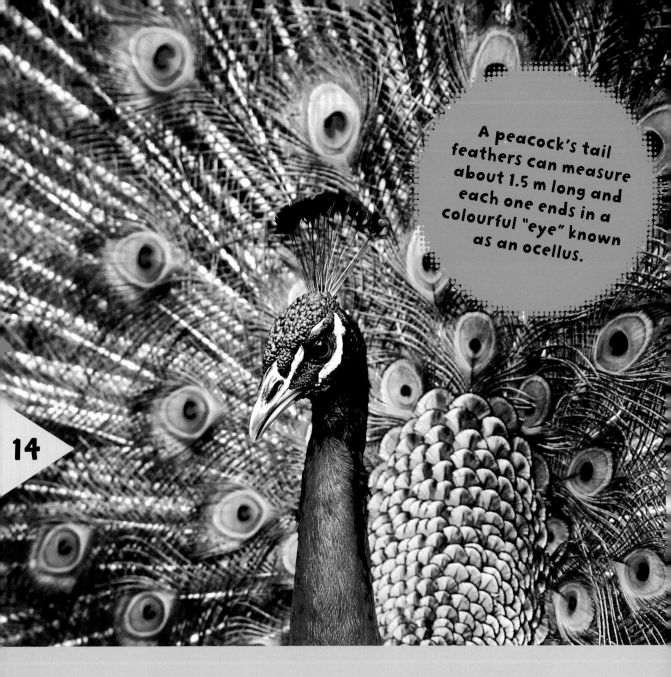

A peacock's tail feathers can measure about 1.5 m long and each one ends in a colourful "eye" known as an ocellus.

14 ▶

It's a peacock!

Mr Fancy-Tail here is a male. He's spreading his feathers in a fan to impress females (peahens). They're grey, but they have an eye for colourful guys!

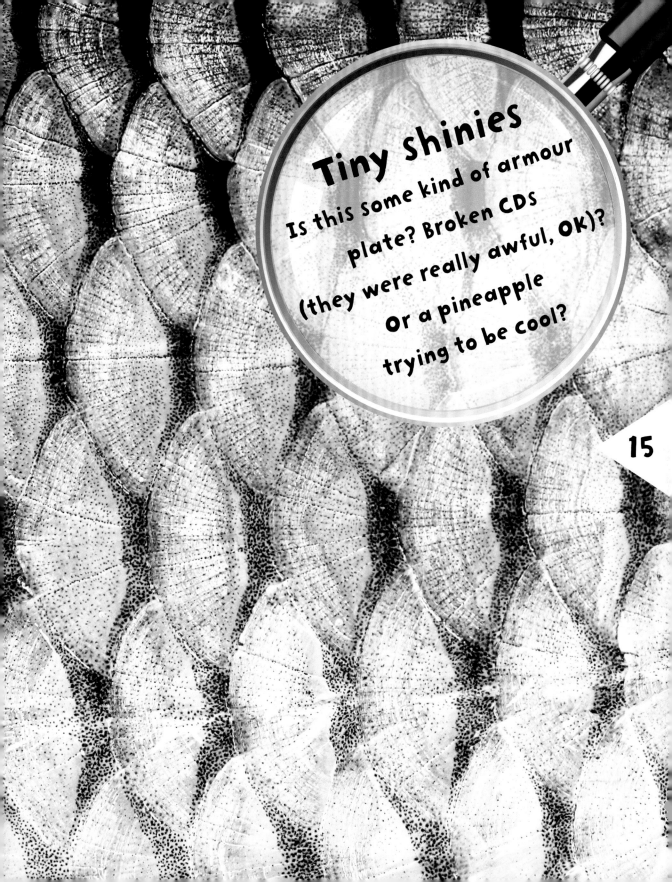

Tiny shinies

Is this some kind of armour plate? Broken CDs (they were really awful, OK)? Or a pineapple trying to be cool?

Some fish can have thousands of scales. Even huge fish like sharks have them. They're just too small for us to see.

16

It's a fish!

Fish bodies are covered with small, shiny scales that overlap and produce a smooth surface. If you grab a live fish, it slips right out of your hands.

Bulgy bobbles and furry fluff

They're all the same kind of object, though. Guess each one, then turn the page.

American football

Basketball

18

Tennis ball

Cricket ball

Obvious, if you just look...
This is quite clearly a bicycle wheel made out of pipe cleaners and a bit of sponge. Isn't it?

It's a dandelion!

Each of the little spinners is a seed, which whirls off through the air in search of a place to put down roots and grow a new plant.

Dandelion seeds can fly up to 5 miles away from the mother plant before finally settling down to grow.

Curled up swirled up

Is this a view inside your body? Or is it the weird outside of someone else's?

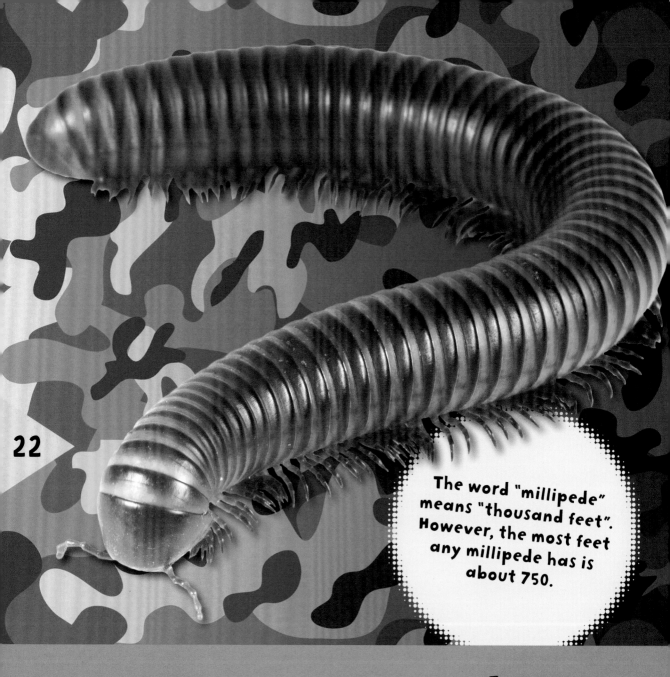

The word "millipede" means "thousand feet". However, the most feet any millipede has is about 750.

It's a millipede!

A millipede has a body that is made up of hundreds of parts called segments. Have you ever held a millipede? It feels like being tickled!

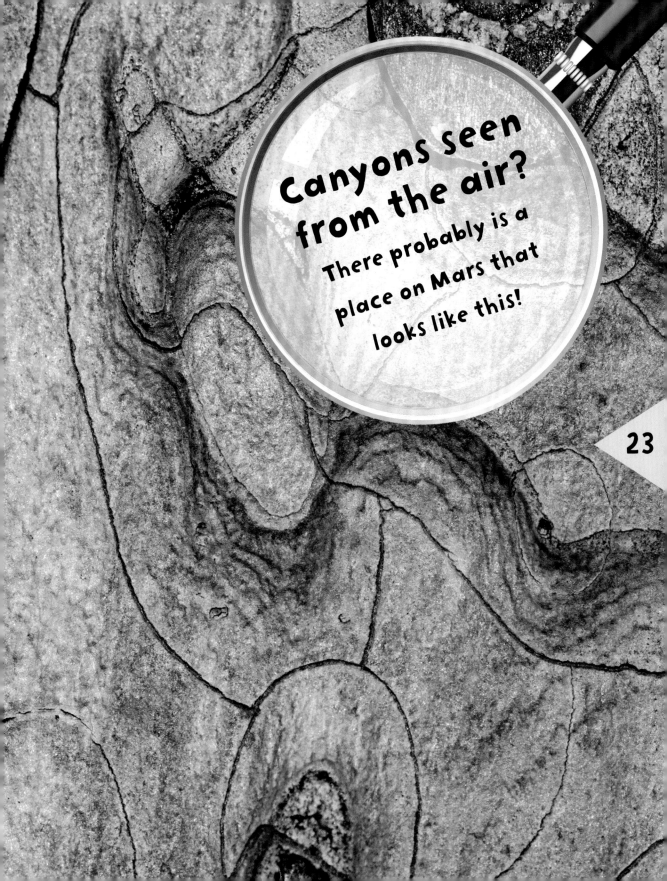

Canyons seen from the air?
There probably is a place on Mars that looks like this!

23

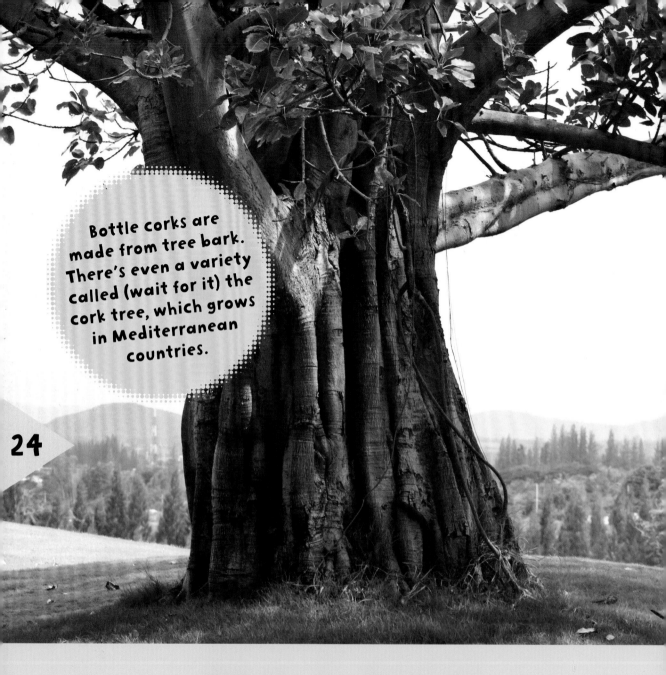

Bottle corks are made from tree bark. There's even a variety called (wait for it) the cork tree, which grows in Mediterranean countries.

It's a tree!

The outside of a tree trunk is covered in tough bark. It's like the tree's version of skin, and protects its insides from getting damaged.

Tree rings,
obviously!
But a tree was the previous
answer...

It's a tortoise!

A tortoise has a shell on its back. It can pull in its head and legs to protect itself from other animals that may want to eat it!

Tortoises can live for a very long time. Some have lived for more than 150 years!

This smells a lot!

Is it part of a leather saddle? A dirty old rag? A really pongy old shoe?

27

A dog's sense of smell can be more than a million times better than yours.

It's a dog's nose!

The tip of a dog's nose is usually wet. This helps it to sniff the air and work out where a smell is coming from.

Can you tell which fruit these pictures show?

Answers at the bottom of page 30.

1
pomegranate
cherries
redcurrants

29

2
plums
grapes
blueberries

3
grapes
apples
limes

4
apples
redcurrants
cherries

30

Stick 'em up!

This looks like a doll having an electric shock. But no plastic people were harmed in the making of this book...

31

Spaghetti comes from the Italian word meaning "thin string".

It's spaghetti!

Spaghetti is long, thin strings of pasta. It's also embarrassment on a plate if you have to eat it in public. Sauce in your hair, on the table, possibly up your nose...

Bumpy, lumpy, veiny...
brain? Hopefully not, with that big gap down the middle.

It's a walnut kernel!

Until 140 years ago you'd have been jumping on your walnuts to try to crack them. The nutcracker was invented in 1878, by Henry Quackenbush.

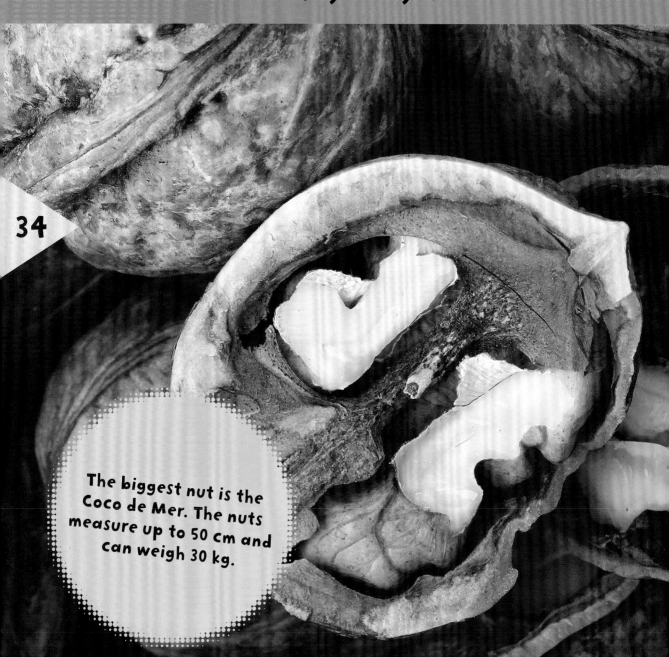

The biggest nut is the Coco de Mer. The nuts measure up to 50 cm and can weigh 30 kg.

It's green!

(We just thought you might need a helpful hint.)

It's a leaf!

These huge leaves are from the banana plant. They're so sturdy and weatherproof that you can build one-storey houses out of them.

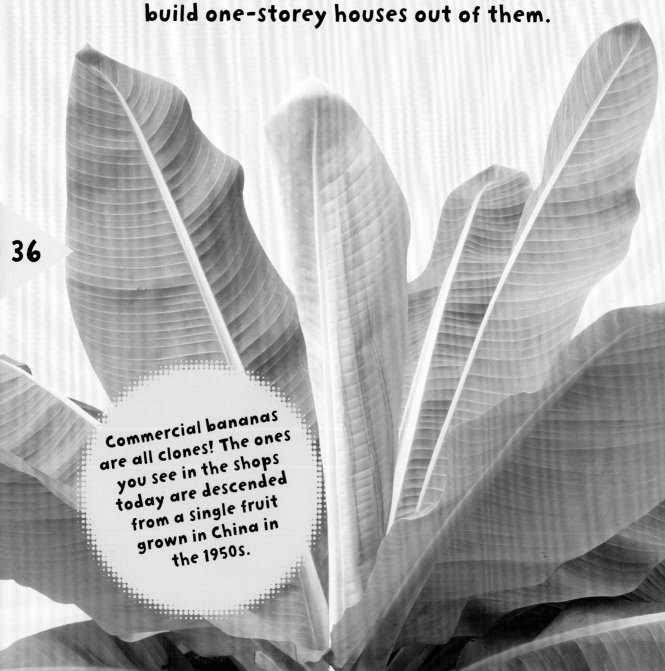

Commercial bananas are all clones! The ones you see in the shops today are descended from a single fruit grown in China in the 1950s.

A whole lot of holes

Is it a bath sponge?
Is it a bubble bath? Or
something wholly
different?

It's bread!

Bread is made of flour and water. If you add yeast too, then the bread 'rises' - bubbles of air appear inside it as it's baked. Light and fluffy!

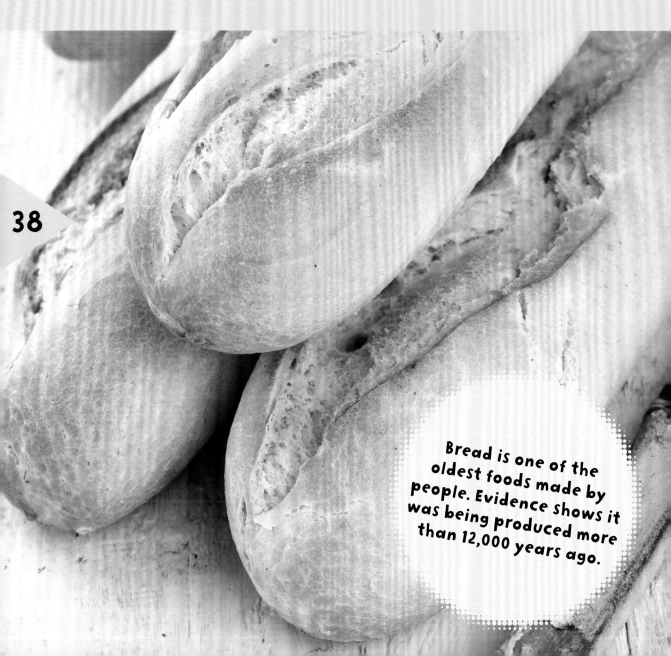

Bread is one of the oldest foods made by people. Evidence shows it was being produced more than 12,000 years ago.

What's this lot?
Grains of coloured sugar?
A microscopic view
of germs having a
family reunion?

It's a carpet!

Carpets are made from threads of material woven together to make a soft surface. Some are pretty luxurious – in 2008 a silk rug sold for $4.5 million!

The idea that red carpets are only for important people is believed to go back to Ancient Greece, when purple and deep red were thought of as the colours of the gods.

1

2

3

41

Different coats for different folks
Who lives inside these skins?
Turn the page to find out.

1
starfish

42

2
polar
bear

3
chameleon

Spiral stumper

Mm, it's a bag of banana flavoured popcorn! Isn't it?

43

It's a sunflower!

Each sunflower can have up to 2,000 seeds in its head. They're often eaten as snacks, or turned into sunflower oil for cooking.

44

The tallest ever sunflower was grown in Germany and measured 8.23 m tall.

45

It's a bag of sweets!
You don't believe it?
All right, so you guessed right
that this is a machine. But
what kind exactly?

The first watches were made more than 500 years ago.

46

It's a watch!

Watches contain a lot of tiny, precise cogs that make the hands move at exactly the right speed.

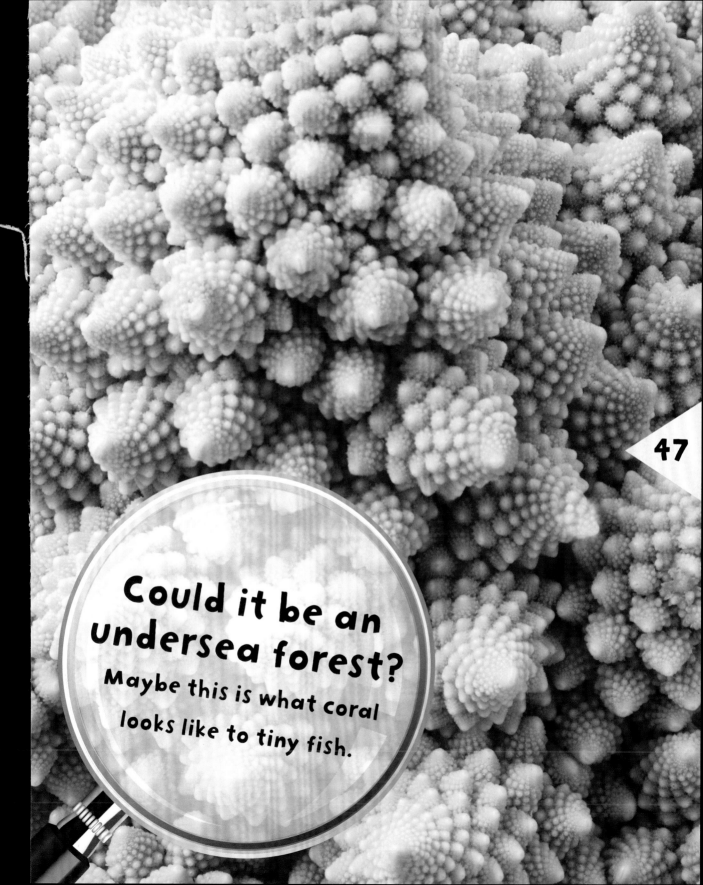

Could it be an undersea forest?
Maybe this is what coral looks like to tiny fish.

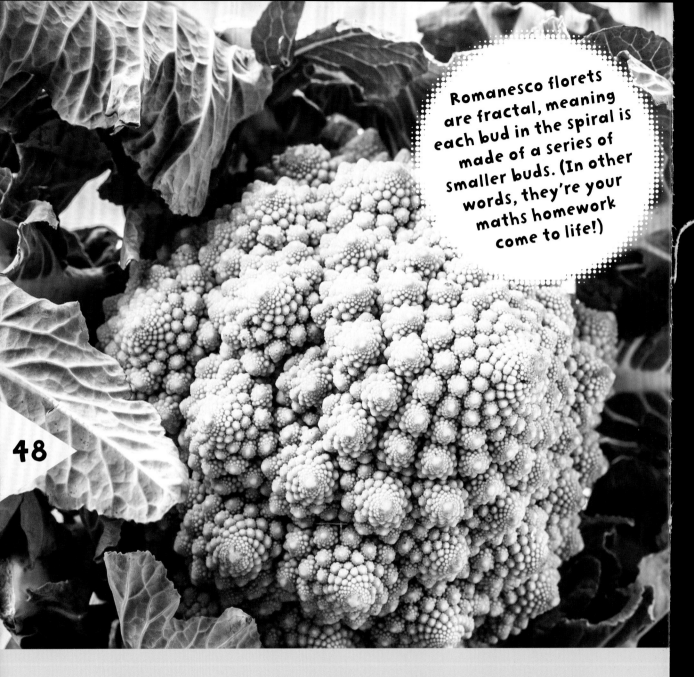

Romanesco florets are fractal, meaning each bud in the spiral is made of a series of smaller buds. (In other words, they're your maths homework come to life!)

It's a cauliflower!

This variety is called Romanesco. It's a genetic cross between cauliflower and broccoli and it tastes nutty. As you might expect!